Soapbox

By Gillian Houghton

Thank you for your support
Gillian Houghton

www.soapsite.biz

Photography and design by J Ottewell
www.souldiva.co.uk

2009 ©

To,

My Father, who taught me never to judge a book by its cover.

'A remarkable man'

My Mother, who shows me how precious life is.

'Truly a lady'

Thank you to those people close enough to love me, support me, understand me and laugh with me.

Especially to Terry for his patience and understanding, Julie for her editing and encouragement (poetry lunches), Gilly for proof reading, James for putting this whole thing together and Amelia *'My Star'*.

Gillian Houghton x

Delicates

"Take Off the Blinkers"

When looking at my photograph,
What do you see?
Does the picture, which only shows the shell,
Really portray me?

If you were to remove my outer casing,
What do you expect to find?
Would you be intrigued to discover,
What is only visible to the blind?

If you were to shut your eyes,
And use your hands to feel.
Would you quickly skim over,
Or enjoy every layer as you peel?

If you were to look into my eyes,
Would you see into my sight?
Would you still be able to see,
If you were to turn out the light?

A video camera for action shots,
Used to play, fast forward or slow.
But this only captures one in time,
And does not let them grow.

A rose petal. A singing bird
Have you seen or really heard.
To stroke, to hug, to really touch,
Learning maybe much too much.

Now when you look at my picture,
What do you see?
Are you creating what you want me to be?
Or accept and see me as simply me?

"Solo"

Drifting towards my dream world,
Solo traveller all alone.
Mind searching and wandering,
Body full-grown.

Seeking evidence and substance,
Contrast of black and white.
Looking deep into the wilderness,
Subconscious seeking sight.

In reality portraying normality,
An existence hard and fast.
Flexibility and infatuation,
Steadfast, unable to grasp.

Demonstration and exhibit,
An illusion never seen.
Solo traveller rambling,
Seeking answers in a dream.

"Distant Dreams"

If I were able to convert my dreams,
I would eagerly set my stage.
Feelings of excitement,
The scene, the script, the page.

Palpitations and speed,
Play acting with greed.
In daylight reminiscing,
Exactly what I am missing.

Entering my vision without stalling,
Stranger's arriving without calling.
Perfection in planting the seed,
Pin pointing emotional need.

Letting loose without any inhibitions,
Racing through without control.
A release rising above myself,
A lost but wandering soul.

Converting dreams into reality,
In the distance I see the stage.
Feelings of excitement,
The scene, the script, the page.

"Mountain Out Of a Molehill"

Men will never understand women,
Until they look inside.
They seem to have been born with the ability,
To emotionally hide.

I'm sure they would be able to open up,
If they decide they would like to look.
Content to go through life; novel in hand,
No inclination to read the book.

Maybe they haven't the ability,
Could it be something they lack?
If they are so hollow,
Why women do they attract?

Many of the times they think with their body,
And do not use their head.
Smiling when they think it appropriate,
Not hearing a word of what's been said.

If they daydream they admit to seeing nothing,
When we do the same we are able to see.
Why is it we are so intrigued?
While they seek peace and to let be.

Not comfortable in coping with emotion and tears,
Unable to face confrontation and fears.
Not brave enough to look inside their own head,
If forced to enter they lightly tread.

We will remain one step ahead,
Of those who once were masters in bed.
Times are changing we are wanting more,
A subject that hits a nerve so raw.

"Choice and Voice"

Having the power of being in control,
Not choosing for anyone to take my reins.
Being able to determine my own happiness,
Having inner strength to muddle through my pain.

It's fine to loosely hold my hand,
To guide me but never force.
A challenge trying to understand my hormones,
And having a partner that can stay the course.

Don't push me too hard as I may jump,
If you order as an animal I may bite.
Just be there to share my joy,
And in darkness provide some light.

Don't be too judgmental: listen and learn,
Who knows what will be round the next corner I turn?
As a friend I am willing to give all,
But I am not amused if I am made a fool.

Don't try to manipulate and mould me,
Although always growing I am at ease.
Even though I seem demanding,
I am not so hard to please.

At times choosing to be out of control,
At times taking tablets to ease my pain.
Choosing to get burnt in the sunshine,
Choosing to get drenched in the rain.

"Penera"

Welcoming you with open arms,
Reflecting warmth as you arrive.
Engulfing you with my presence,
Relaxing, your spirits rise.

Unwinding and reviving,
Feeling secure and safe.
Body slowly thawing,
This is your special place.

Encouraging laughter,
Scene of beauty so surreal.
Pinching yourself periodically,
Proving what you feel is real.

I offer you the seashore,
The softness of the sand.
Taking time to walk with you,
Gently caressing your hand.

Extending my hospitality,
I indulge you with a breeze.
Moments constantly measured,
Not wanting you to leave.

I am your destination,
A quiet haven to chill.
Visits becoming frequent,
Because of how I make you feel.

Persistent in departure,
I'm certain you'll be back.
Reality in returning home,
But in your heart I hold your hat.

"Underground Encounters"

Bodies all around me,
Communication nil.
Bullish behaviour,
Unwilling to reveal.

Privacy and peculiarity,
Open but blind.
No inclination,
To discover and find.

Facial expressions,
To smile or frown.
Standing high,
Looking down.

Shyness or surety,
Warned to keep clear.
Our bodies are touching,
So far but so near.

Interruptions encountered,
Boarding or embark.
Travelling in daytime,
Internally dark.

Familiarity in person,
Seeing you every day.
Robots on route,
Seeking pay.

Packed like sardines,
Uninvited entering space.
Too close for comfort,
Face to face.

"Mucked Up"

Madness a moment,
A moment too soon.
Staying up late,
To watch the moon.

Talking to myself,
Answering too.
Wanting to be normal,
What can I do?

Sleeping in the daytime,
Awake at night.
Internally unable to control,
The continuous fight.

To whimper to wander,
Round and about.
To loose control,
Scream & shout.

Mucked up and drugged up,
An attempt to stable,
Will I sustain?
Will I be able?

"Grateful"

I am so grateful for your kindness,
When I felt so scared and alone.
The kindness that you showed me,
Is not portrayed in your appearance or tone.

Your patience and determination,
Really saved my day.
I put all my faith in you,
As you confidently led the way.

I held on to you so tight,
As you struggled to breathe.
You could have turned your back on me,
Taking no responsibility and to leave.

I thanked you in drunken stupor,
Because I felt so small.
However, I have never forgotten your kindness,
That day you were my all.

"Sunshine & Rain"

A release, a breakdown,
Pulling you down to your knees.
All systems have stopped,
No longer able to weave.

A mind war, a halt,
On this no lesson has been taught.
A muddle, a mess,
Unable to put on my dress.

An overpowering sensation,
No control of direction.
Not necessarily from,
Physical or mental rejection.

Demanding lifestyles,
Emotions on hold.
Fed up with doing what's expected,
Or what you are told.

How far to the edge,
Are we standing sane?
Convincing ourselves of sunshine,
When there is clearly rain.

"Good Friends"

Friendship formed in the good times,
Hand holding when times got bad.
Encouraging me to relax and enjoy,
When I felt depressed and sad.

You showed me understanding,
When the going got too tough.
Remaining positive and patient,
Having heard more than enough.

Concocting conversations,
When I was too upset to speak.
Pointing out the sunshine,
When I was cold and bleak.

Remaining by my side,
When I felt so alone.
Always offering advice,
At the end of the phone.

Discreetly holding a torch,
When I stood destitute in darkness.
Showing understanding,
When I sought forgiveness.

Trustworthy and reliable,
An honour you're my friend.
Appreciation,
Able to depend.

"Our Time - Our Space"

Tonight is special,
Strictly for the girls.
Rebellious maybe raunchy,
No ribbons and curls.

Girls behaving badly,
Aggressively allure.
Cheshire cat,
Seductively purr.

Calculated conspiracy,
Messing with the mind.
Synchronising movements,
Finger on rewind.

Confident performance,
Dangerously dance.
Taking no prisoners,
No second chance.

Revelations and secrets,
All to be revealed.
Intuition and intrusion,
Moments wrapped and sealed.

"VIP"

I don't need three letters,
To say what I was born to be.
I don't need a title on a name badge,
For all and sundry to read and see.

I don't require such recognition,
From those too far from me to care.
I don't need a designer outfit,
Or instructions what to wear.

I am not seeking attention,
Comfortable to mingle with the crowd.
Choosing to step back and observe,
When others are excitable and loud.

Don't engage with me in conversation,
Because it may do you good.
Don't try to control me,
Because you thought you could.

"Spin The Wheel"

Cameras watching my every move,
A roulette table, time to choose.
Spinning the wheel, excitement pending,
Overdrawn, physically spending.

Mind over matter,
Master and skill.
Gambling mayhem,
Placing a deal.

Dangerously addicting,
Fun and games.
Destitution,
Staying sane.

High emotions,
Getting a buzz.
Deceit and lies,
To the one you love.

Learning a lesson,
What's been taught?
Silently struggling,
Trapped and caught.

"Lightening"

Unable to hide from my conscience,
Yearning to wipe the slate clean.
Unable to erase,
What my eyes have seen.

Uncomfortable looking in the mirror,
Confronted with what I've become.
Hiding behind a thundercloud,
Resenting the sun.

Frustrated at the pleasures,
That I witnessed taking place.
Visions of togetherness,
Always in my face.

Intrusion in illusion,
Distantly involved.
Solutions at stalemate,
Unable to resolve.

"Out Of Touch"

Missing you so much,
Wishing you was here.
Short lived laughter,
Camouflage a tear.

Testing telephone calls,
Whispering words, sincere.
Misinterpretation,
Not always clear.

Travelling far and wide,
Places I've never been.
Exciting experiences,
Living 'your dream'.

Distance now dangerous,
Out of control.
Unable to touch you,
As you stand in goal.

Communication breakdown,
Our future's been blown.
Back to reality,
I stand - alone.

"A Moment's Peace"

An open space,
This space is mine.
An empty bottle,
A glass of wine.

This place is for me,
Do not come near.
An empty glass,
A bottle of beer.

No height restrictions,
So much room up above.
A champagne bottle,
To think of love.

It's no time to share,
Nothing to give away.
A waiter passing,
An empty tray.

"Why am I not welcome"?
I hear you say.
Although a full menu,
No bill to pay.

This place is quiet,
Extremely remote.
No hat stand,
Or hook to hang your coat.

No bus stops or taxis
Just the air, space and me.
Complete for this moment,
The way I want it to be.

"Teardrops"

So many tears,
Different people cry.
My eye spotting upset,
Why is it only I?

To comfort and listen,
A friendly cuddle.
Compassion shown,
Such a muddle.

Work problems,
Near and dear.
To advise and direct,
To manoeuvre and steer.

Personal problems,
A secret to keep.
Behind the curtains,
Allowed to peep.

Relationship downfalls,
Love and hate.
Being truthful enough,
To admit a mistake.

To be direct and honest,
Up front but to care.
How many uniforms,
Am I able to wear?

"Precious Moments"

Thanks for the moment,
A moment of your time.
Time that is precious,
Precious possession of mine.

Grateful for your words of wisdom,
Wisdom that comes with age.
Age an advantage in the art of learning,
Learning how to deal with joy and pain.

Kindness that you show to me,
Am I worthy of such action?
Action that comes from the heart,
Heart beating faster at an initial attraction.

Loving and listening,
Listening to what I say.
Saying sometimes far too much,
Much time I am made to pay.

"Streets lined with gold"

London – it really is my London,
Wherever I am, it always will be.
Knowing it like the back of my hand,
As an outsider would never be able to see.

Inner city and so picturesque,
Victorian houses so tall.
My childhood memories are the best,
I really had it all.

Our playground was the street,
Parked cars and litter.
We were often called street urchins,
It amuses me at such ignorance, I'm not bitter.

Learning the art of how to communicate with others,
To find amusement in play and to share.
Always encouraged to have respect for your elders,
Helping elderly neighbours, be courteous and to care.

A game of knock down ginger, always was a winner,
Hitting the jackpot if you disturbed their dinner.
Being chased, feeling scared, but this would entice you back,
Not understanding a sense of humour that adults sometimes lack.

Girl Guides and Brownies,
Cubs and Scouts.
Sunday morning church parade,
Always well turned out.

Primary schools and secondary schools,
State school the only choice.
Getting on with education,
No hard feelings to voice.

To be taught that anything could be achieved,
Through dedication and hard work.
Having the edge, being street wise,
Was a valued added perk.

London, My London,
Was it through progress you changed?
Now living just outside you,
Feeling sometimes strange.

Colours

"Fancy Dress"

Who really are you?
Would you dare ask?
This would mean being brave,
And taking off your mask.

Sit in front of the mirror,
Starting first with your eyes.
No mascara to enhance them,
Are they telling you lies?

You rely on your eyes,
To sort the bad out from the good.
Occasionally reporting back a masterpiece,
Mistaking a piece of rotting wood.

Your nose a shapely feature,
It's purpose being smell.
Trained to pick up certain scent,
And if attractive, may ring your bell.

Look in the mirror at the wrapping you see,
What you see, do you want to be?
Have you got the determination to change,
Something that took so long to arrange?

Will you revert back to the mask,
That has been structured over many years?
The same mask that has protected,
The eye from so many tears.

The same mask can be your enemy,
As well as your friend.
The same mask can be destroyed,
No longer willing to pretend.

"Invasion of space"

To be weak,
To be strong.
To be right,
To be wrong.

To elaborate,
To fabricate.
To congratulate,
To manipulate.

To confuse,
To abuse.
To win,
To lose.

To wait,
Be patient.
A longing,
Of belonging.

To question,
To answer.
To avoid,
To master.

To try,
To let.
To want,
To get.

To achieve,
To grieve.
To stay,
To leave.

"Tasting"

Interesting and appealing,
Suitable to the taste.
Admiring from afar,
Must not act in haste.

Gathering and mastering,
The texture depth and shape.
Measurements mentally taken,
No requirements for a ruler or tape.

Sampling the merchandise,
Enjoying the process.
Having had the experience,
Do you think anything less?

Thinking of others,
In which to compare.
Will you be committed?
Would you ever dare?

Talk of and learn,
Take note and to turn.
Indulge or disregard,
Decisions, incredibly hard.

"Lilo"

Your fantasy alarms me,
I respect it all the same.
This experience unfortunately,
Will not erase a lifetime's pain.

Although you have been damaged,
And you feel the wounds will never heal.
This is a part of your make-up,
And what makes you so real.

Your experiences are priceless,
Look for the happiness amongst the pain.
Don't let the hurt keep reappearing,
As it will emotionally drain.

You are an exceptional person,
With the ability to listen and give advice.
Our friendship to me,
Is without a price.

You have grown into something greater,
Than those who failed you, could ever achieve.
But getting back to this fantasy,
Let me know before you leave.

"Take my hand"

Don't be scared little one,
Come to me.
I have the ability to see,
What the eye cannot always see.

I know you are hurting,
I can feel your pain.
Although there is sunshine,
I can see the rain.

Let me touch you,
Let go of your pride.
Let loose your anger,
And what you are trying to hide.

Lost in a tunnel in darkness,
I am armed with a torch to provide light.
I will join forces with you,
If you want to continue to fight.

Together we can watch the flowers grow,
Your problems halved, now that I know.
Faced again with another day,
Have you faith in what I say?

"Timing"

I'm sorry that you are hurting,
But I cannot ease your pain.
I'm sure it's a comfort,
Knowing that I too am caught in the rain.

Greedy for the sunshine,
Buying it by the pound.
Delaying the settlement payment,
Watching the water hit the ground.

Digging deep to get out of a hole,
Burying your head underground like a mole.
Unfortunately on the surface all is not bright,
Kicking yourself for having no foresight.

Share the experience of the feeling
That you felt as your fingers burnt.
The most important thing right now,
Is if the lesson has been learnt.

Trapped in a corner,
No energy left to attack.
Feeling like a failure,
Confidence now lacks.

You must hold your head up high,
As you withdraw and admit defeat.
Keep your head down and pen poised,
Wait for the right time to retreat.

"Surprised"

I think I have found you,
Although you expertly hide.
Knowing where you're coming from,
Be assured I'm by your side.

Withdrawal from reality,
In a situation wrong.
You now have an ally,
Having waited for so long.

Discussions and opinions,
Battle with the facts.
To be in agreement,
Substance sometimes lacks.

Honesty spells progression,
Stepping closer towards the dream.
A friend who's not pretentious,
A shoulder for you to lean.

"Unlock the Box"

You describe yourself as an empty box,
Decorated in shiny paper and a bow.
Although you portray being happy and high,
You say you feel worn out and low.

I know you want to delve inside,
And discover what is there.
Sadly many simply judge,
By the wrapping that you wear.

I'm listening to the heartbeat,
The rhythm of the song.
I want to change the tune for you,
I know you have waited for so long.

You know that something is missing,
You are aware of this I know.
Why are you afraid to enter,
Where you really want to go?

Break loose from the paper,
Start to fill your box.
No more chains to restrict you,
No key or safety lock.

35

"PYO"

Bearing fruit,
Blossom and grow.
How much about you,
Does he know?

Handling the merchandise,
Evaluate and weigh.
Wistfully thinking,
Made to pay.

Experience the flavours,
Taste buds pleased.
Half eaten,
Stopping to tease.

Fruit for hunger,
Juice for thirst.
Anticipation,
Ready to burst.

"Love Triangle"

You are adamant that you still love him,
Although you must, you don't want to let him go.
The relationship must come to an end,
For your own sanity, this you know.

Even though the links are tight,
You must cut loose from the chain.
Short term it will hurt so much,
Abort the good times from your brain.

To finalise the arrangement,
Will allow you to move ahead.
How fair are you being,
To the man with whom you share your bed?

Trapped in a love triangle situation,
But you know that three is a crowd.
Although you could accept sunshine,
You keep enticing the cloud.

Different qualities to offer, contributing to your life,
It was you who decided you didn't want to be his wife.
How fair are you being to the third party, dangling him on a string?
Why can't you accept the happiness that to you he could bring.

Is this a way of punishing yourself,
For experiencing failure in your life.
The vows can always be re-said,
If your vocation is to be his wife.

37

"Pen to paper"

I dare you to write a letter,
Divulge in words how you feel.
A brave face is not a requirement,
To be truthful and real.

Try to express your deepest thoughts,
Take time to sit and write.
The paper is an open space,
The pen a string and kite.

You don't have to send what has been said,
A way to unload but lightly tread.
Writing connects your heart with your head,
It's your prerogative if it is read.

"Self-built"

Ask yourself what you are doing,
Do you know what it's all about?
Is it driven by pent up anger?
Do you silently scream and shout?

Prosperity and honesty,
Honest to me or you.
You don't appear relaxed and at ease,
With what you are choosing to do.

An anagram that can't be solved,
Lacking the clues to complete the task.
An itch you are unable to scratch,
But far too proud to ask.

Providing others with guidance,
Your own puzzle still incomplete.
Are you looking for compensation?
Or is it an achievement to be discreet?

Outside portraying being able,
But inside you crumble as we speak.
Your castle that was once so strong,
Is now fragile and weak.

Ascertain your objectives,
Find the strength that once drove you on.
Sometimes being right,
Can also be so wrong.

"Mixed Emotions"

A mixing bowl - a wooden spoon
The sunshine - an evening moon.

The ingredients must be just right
An evening breeze, a day so bright

Salt replacing sugar would ruin the bake
The birds that sing, the noise they make.

Sultanas or raisins, does it matter
The dogs that bark, how they like to chatter.

The temperature must be just so
It's amazing how small babies grow.

The end result, is it as expected?
It's heartbreaking how some are rejected.

A wire tray to let it cool
A little mouth that likes to drool.

A little now and more for later
A gift of life could not be greater.

"The Generation Gap"

A grandfather. A grandson,
A generation missing.
Proudly standing side by side,
Both in thought and wishing.

Hand in hand, one large, one small,
One so little, the other not so tall.
Story telling, no need for yelling,
Always exciting, the memory writing.

Old money, new money,
It's all about timing.
Pound notes once in the pocket,
Now there's a hole in the lining.

Looking up to, looking down at,
Willing each other to continue to grow.
Winding up and winding down,
So fast and almost slow.

Energetic and moving fast,
The body struggling, but trying to last.
To teach with ease, so much patience,
The body however, requiring maintenance.

Lines in his face,
Could write a book.
Looking at each other,
An admiring look.

"Fair Value"

Markets for trading,
What do you sell?
Reveal the secret of your success,
Please enlighten and tell.

Ups and downs,
Figures and facts.
Keeping calm in chaos,
With dignity react.

One price for selling,
Another to buy.
Up front and honesty,
Detecting a lie.

Buyers and sellers,
Name your price.
Looking attractive,
Sure to entice.

Facts and figures,
Straight up and not faking.
Value for money,
Or are you profit taking?

"Essence"

Calculated contentment,
Naturally at ease.
Exterior laughing,
Emotionally pleased.

Dates and destinations,
Spending quality time.
Time to observe,
The warning signs.

Talk and listen,
Listen and learn.
Forward thinking,
Goalposts turn.

Adoring the pattern,
The colour now bores.
Opportunities calling,
Closing doors.

Doormats and deadlines,
Wiping your feet.
Maker and master,
Destined to meet.

43

"Too good to be true"

Today you opened and revealed your plans,
The future for you looking bright.
It's nice to see your excitement,
For something that's only 'a might'.

You have gone back to basics,
And will not be swayed.
By a fancy job title,
And a little extra pay.

You know what you want,
I once wanted it too.
But I'm the unlucky one,
I will really miss you.

Your life in a bubble,
Influenced by your faith.
Angels to protect you,
Feeling always so safe.

"Stand at ease"

Stand to attention or stand at ease,
Who really are you trying to please?
Orders and actions, action for what,
What are you giving, what have you got?

Don't take for granted I'm selling,
It's my market and my choice.
What are you saying, stop that whispering,
Is it because of shyness you are afraid to voice?

Taking or giving or do you give to take?
Questions asked, decisions to make.
Answer without hesitation or stall for time,
You must know if you are mine.

Mind over matter, matter of fact,
The chemistry calling, to initially attract.
Attraction and reaction - love or hate,
Are you making a big mistake?

"Colour Blind"

When I am thinking ahead,
The colour is red.
Why do I see blue?
When I am thinking of you.

To me red indicates danger,
Excitement and thrills.
Blue is cold and boring,
Mortgage payments and bills.

Green being tranquil,
Stimulating the mind.
White indicates pure,
An incredible find.

Burnt orange, palpitations,
A fast beating heart.
Already providing warmth,
A positive start.

Maybe yellow is required,
Springtime and daffodils.
Black is for thunderclouds,
Legislation and wills.

A painting of splattered colour,
No feature, a mess, but bright.
A frame controlling the chaos,
To test the mind and sight.

A picture hook for stability,
Hung for all to see.
Looking at this picture,
It could resemble me.

"Hold on in there"

Exterior quiet and shy,
But different when he's with you.
Having been at first base for so long,
What next together will you do?

Commitment - not in writing,
Or by the giving of a ring.
Hiding behind his music,
But not so keen to sing.

Fully aware of what you want,
Maybe unconsciously he wants it too.
But scared of getting it wrong,
And being a failure to himself and you.

If you don't give, you are not faced with rejection,
As rejection can knock you to your knees.
Happy living under the same roof,
And if disappointed you can leave.

Childhood memories not so exciting,
Although loved, the family home not so inviting.
Strange and stranger, cuddle or cuddled,
Surviving but growing up emotionally muddled.

Still his hand needs to be held,
But also needing space to be alone.
Although an adult he is still learning,
Like us all he's not full grown.

Children are a huge responsibility,
His expectations of himself are high.
Not 100 per cent knowing his reasons for denying you,
And when feeling brave asks himself why.

What does he really want?
Maybe he is too scared to say.
Still you are there proving your love for him,
Determined not to let him drive you away.

Whites

"Security blanket"

I think about you often,
You are always on my mind.
In my heart you are still with me,
And never left behind.

From up above you witness my ups and downs,
Probably at times nodding your head.
I know you are not far away from me,
At night as I lay in bed.

You taught me about love and discipline,
So many cuddles and hugs.
I will never let you go,
You are my very own personal rug.

Keeping me warm when I get cold,
Showing its age as it gets old.
The pattern sometimes hard to see,
But no one can see it, only me.

"Give me back what I had"

Why did you leave me,
I was so young and naïve?
I wasn't even sure,
How I was meant to grieve.

When you lay there struggling,
Were you deciding to live or die?
Why did you let death pull you towards it,
Or did you not have the strength to try?

You always said I was your little girl,
And I loved to be just that.
I was so very proud of you,
And that's an honest fact.

You would not have to say anything,
To be chastised would only require a look.
Many hours you would sit in a chair,
With your head stuck in a book.

Did you know mum always covered for me,
When I would arrive home late?
You didn't like the thought of me growing up,
And actually having a date.

Your wit so dry,
Your magnetism drawing others near,
The laughter in your company,
Often brought a tear.

You always kissed me in the morning,
And in the evening when it was time for bed.
Many never experience such love and affection,
I'm trying to follow in the footsteps that you led.

Mum left without a husband,
Me left without my Dad.
I still cannot accept it,
I want back what I had.

I would love to put my arms around you,
And turn back time.
I would never let you go,
To ensure you would always be there and be mine.

Dad I would just love to speak to you,
To update you on what you have missed.
It would also be nice to touch you,
And if you had to go – give you a farewell kiss.

"Dad"

A Father, a Man, a Giant, a Mouse,
Usually the one that rules the house.

To look up at, to look down at,
To curse at, to frown at.

To love, to cuddle, a kiss, a look,
You could never define him in a book.

A mountain, an oak tree
As dependable as can be.

A man, a parent, a husband a son,
Until a time his work is done.

A memory, an honour to have had,
The pleasure of having such a wonderful Dad.

"Mum"

My mother, his wife, most certainly a lady.
Will I grow to be like her, I hope so, maybe.
So precious, so kind,
So clever in mind.

The sunshine, the rain
The love, the pain.
A teardrop, a sad look,
A lifetime, a good book.

To learn from, so forgiving,
Life is for living.
To be here, to be there,
Always to care.

To fall back on, to rely on,
And always depend on.
To sacrifice for you,
A love so true.

She, the one to defend,
A tear she will mend.
As fragile as a petal,
As tough as metal.

To love, to teach,
A walk on the beach.
To throw pebbles that sink,
An eyelash, a wink.

To love, respect,
Learn from and admire.
In her old age I sit
And watch her tire.

An afternoon snooze,
No time to lose.
Recharge the batteries, set the speed,
Continuing to pull out the unwanted weeds.

A mother, my mother, and most definitely a lady,
Will I be like her, I hope so, maybe.

"Live & Learn"

I can't think of life without you,
You are one on your own.
It is through your love and guidance,
That I have grown.

I know you are very proud of me,
I sometimes wonder why.
You put me on a pedestal,
Standing up so very high.

In the role that you play,
You provide more than I need.
I'm always looking for something more,
Living a life led by want and greed.

Greedy for material things,
That I know deep down mean nothing.
My life is an act of confidence,
And the art to keep on bluffing.

You are so innocent and real,
Full of emotions and so kind.
Sometimes I don't see in front of me,
My eyes don't see but blind.

I hope I learn from my mistakes,
And turn out just to be.
A carbon copy of you,
But not you, me.

"All That I Ask"

Will you come back,
Are you still there?
Do you have the ability
To still care?

Do you have feelings of old,
Are you tired and cold?
Are you settled in time,
Are you still mine?

Can you remember that something special we had,
Does the distance make you feel sad?
Or are you content,
And glad you were sent?

Can you hear the blackbirds that sing?
Can you hear the church bells that ring?
Can you answer the questions I ask?
Or is it an impossible task?

I still remember the taste of your kiss,
In my heart you are still missed.

"In your shadow"

I can't help but notice her standing there,
Intrigued by the happiness in her eyes.
Coming to life as she looks at you,
Heart on her sleeve, no disguise.

She looks so young and carefree,
In a classic floral dress.
Many miles and moons away,
From any darkness or distress.

Walking through fields of forever,
Resting by a shallow stream.
Singing songs of yesterday,
Entering your dream.

Watching you as you try to sum up,
Why life can be so unfair.
She is always in your shadow,
Although you are unaware.

"Loop the Loop"

More is always going on,
Than you will be able to see.
What really are my qualities?
What do you see in me?

Hormonal changes and mood swings,
Were you born with a pair of wings?
Remaining patient and understanding,
A turbulent flight, but a smooth landing.

If you are right, I'll make you wrong,
If I'm wrong, I'm always right.
Mastering the art of confusion,
But guaranteed a fight.

In a maze I'll lose you,
Expert at hiding, but not running away.
Facing responsibilities in my own time,
But taking on board what you say.

Although more is often going on,
Than the eye can see.
Are you enjoying this rollercoaster ride,
That you choose to share with me?

"Wanting and Getting"

I want to award you with my kisses,
I want to knight you with my touch.
I want to hold you so close to me,
And to tell you I love you so much.

I want to hold your hand,
And squeeze it until you cry,
I want to take you places,
Where such pleasure makes you high.

I want us to go so deep together,
That no other person has been.
I want our eyes to experience,
What no other person has seen.

I want to walk towards the sunset,
Until we meet the moon.
I want us to hibernate,
Protected by a cocoon.

I want to be on a desert island,
Just to have you for myself.
Material things no importance,
And our love to be our wealth.

"Take note"

So loving, your eyes sparkling,
As you really look.
A hardback novel,
Not a paperback book.

To touch with feeling,
To admire, to stare.
A warmth, a knowing,
That you care.

To lie alongside,
A cuddle, such meaning,
Am I awake?
Am I dreaming?

To respect as a person,
A best friend, a lover.
Where would we be
Without each other?

To laugh, a giggle,
A joke, a remark.
The feeling inside,
A fast beating heart.

A pair, a soul mate,
You know what I think.
Feeling so special,
As you give me a wink.

A smile, the memory,
A lovely weekend.
A pity these two days,
Have had to end.

"A Cuddle"

To lay along side you after an argument,
Adamant that I don't touch.
Insides turning over,
Hurting so much.

Moving across my foot,
To slightly touch yours.
Taking my time,
Relaxing my claws.

As sleep sets in,
The body takes over.
Moving together,
Getting closer.

Relaxing, a great comfort,
A peace from within.
Although no entertainment,
A definite win.

To be close – To touch,
The feel of your skin.
The security of loving,
The excitement you bring.

It has not got to be sexual,
But comfort in feeling safe.
Held together relaxed,
A special place.

"Context"

Night-time niceties,
Daytime dreams.
Mixed emotions,
Ancient has beens.

Darkness and danger,
Pulling me close.
Reality in reasoning,
Expectations rose.

Brightness and beauty,
Sensing the truth.
Emotionally revealing,
Acting aloof.

Afternoon siesta,
Savour and steal.
Heart rendering,
Questioning real.

Ripeness and reality,
Experiencing ware.
Misty mornings,
Knowing you care.

"Appreciation"

You brighten each day,
Provide protection at night.
You represent the sunshine,
In darkness my light.

You encourage me to smile,
When I'm feeling bad.
You remind me of the good times,
When I am feeling sad.

You are there to comfort me,
In each set back and every tear.
It's a personal achievement,
Keeping you interested to stay near.

When I am too angry to speak,
You encourage conversation.
Willing to be my punch bag,
To relieve my frustration.

You brighten each corner,
Of every room in which you walk.
Having the ability to,
Love, listen and talk.

"Not Yet"

Don't give up on our journey,
I'm asking you not to leave.
I'm not strong enough at this moment,
To be able to sanely grieve.

Stay a little longer,
Hold tightly to my hand.
Let us one more time,
Carve our initials in the sand.

I need to smile a few more times,
It would be good again to laugh.
Short term the requirement is a full measure,
It's not a time to be giving halves.

I'm waiting to collect your hugs,
To be held so tight so I can't breathe.
For you to look at me in that certain way,
You know the way you tease.

In time I may have to let you go,
Gradually to loosen my grip.
At this time I admit I'm not ready,
To experience the final trip.

"Splitting Hairs"

Your love is suffocating me,
I am struggling to breathe.
If you refuse to release your grip,
I may run away and leave.

You once loved me for my individuality,
Now you're determined to strip me bare.
Demanding all my attention,
Assuming that I care.

Snuggling up close as I lay in bed,
I'd like to experience a little space.
Choosing to lie back to back,
Once content face to face.

Feeling restrained and uncomfortable,
From you I'm breaking free.
Determined to be my own person,
No longer prepared to say we.

"For Keeps"

I've never thought of you as baggage,
But only as a priceless gift.
An image of you in my head,
My spirits automatically lift.

Perfection not an illusion,
A lifetime achievement and reward.
Thanking nature for nurture,
Accepting a present from the Lord.

Although still growing oblivious,
To what awaits you outside.
There is an army waiting to protect you,
Always there and on your side.

Each day is another milestone,
Feet wearily soldiering on.
Trying to give the best to you,
Together learning right from wrong.

Unsure if we will complete this journey,
But each day's special and you're mine.
Reading my body and responding,
Looking for only positive signs.

Each moment is an encounter,
I'm looking forward to tomorrow.
Achieving a little more each day,
Full of happiness not sorrow.

"Amelia - Born To Be..."

Little lady you are going to be a star,
Everyone will know exactly who you are.
Eventually when you hit the big time,
Relax as everything will be just fine.
You have that special something,
A certain magic that makes you, you.
You will know exactly where you are going,
You will know exactly what to do.

I have seen the stars twinkle in your presence,
So high up and looking down.
Always there to provide direction,
In rhythm moving to your sound.
Also the sun demands a part of you,
Smiling in the distance enhancing your glow.
Thunder and lightening providing direction,
Warning you when you are too high or low.

Your beauty will always capture,
The attention of the crowd.
Your character compelling,
Fun – respectful – loud.
A love for life, so many things to do,
Whatever, whenever I'll be watching you.
A star, a shining, born to be,
Sit back, enjoy, watch and see.

Woollens

"A stitch in time"

What makes you tick?
What's in your head?
Are you a leader?
Are you being led?

Do you think of bad things,
That you know are wrong?
Are you feeling all alone,
As if you don't belong?

Is there a special person,
In which you can reveal?
All the things you are thinking,
Are they really real?

Do you shut your eyes and see things,
That you feel they shouldn't see?
Does anyone keep appearing,
Is that person me?

Do you gaze at the stars?
Look deep into the moon?
Are you planning a journey,
Is there any room?

Do you wish and wonder,
What life will become?
Do you stand tall and wait,
Do you panic and run?

Are you a holly bush,
So sharp to keep all at bay?
Are you a tulip in full bloom,
And in the wind will sway?

What makes you excited?
What do you expect?
Are you content,
Or living with regret?

"A piece of string"

Malicious and menacing,
Choosing to manipulate.
Unable to be open,
So you blindly make mistakes.

Don't show me the side I want to see,
If there's another side to the coin.
I need to study the whole picture,
Before deciding to join.

Don't be smarmy and smile,
When you really want to frown.
Don't treat me like royalty,
And present me with a crown.

Respect me for my intelligence,
For the characteristics that make me - me.
Don't treat me as a possession,
For all and sundry to judge and see.

Don't twist and turn issues,
To confuse the debate.
Don't feel guilty about disliking me,
Love runs parallel to hate.

Don't stroke and comfort me,
If you plan to strike and scold.
Or feel guilty of being with me today,
If you don't plan with me to grow old.

After choosing me you may lose me,
If the quality is poor.
Having satisfied our hunger on the apple,
Is there any interest in the core?

72

"999"

I'm really not missing you,
Relaxed in loosening my ties.
A relief having to listen to,
Familiar tales and lies.

Bored and bewildered,
Corporate smiles so false.
Having completed the race,
Now unsure of the course.

Trading and parading,
Enticed to buy what I sell.
Once enjoyable and challenging,
Now stagnating in hell.

"Natures Way"

Secretive squirrel,
Hiding its find.
Intellectual planning,
Challenging the mind.

Wise owl wondering,
Seeking its prey.
Superiority,
Leading the way.

Hedgehog weary,
Prickly heat.
Developing goose bumps,
Sharp but weak.

Wise and wonderful,
Secrets to keep.
Dicing with nature,
Digging deep.

"His"

Inability to understand yourself,
So how can you understand her?
Mind misled and scrambled,
Outbursts too often occur.

Possessive of her person,
But liking others to look.
Clothes sometimes enticing,
The bait, a line and hook.

It was her outgoing personality,
Which intrigued you to pursue.
Now you calculate the attention,
Given to others compared with you.

Popularity versus insecurity,
Characteristics strong or weak.
It's time to look inside your head,
To find the answers that you seek.

Misleading in the melody,
Unable to grasp the language of love.
Out of body experience,
Look down from up above.

"Busy line"

All or nothing,
What exactly have you got?
The truth is you have nothing,
But you think you have the lot.

You appear to lack a conscience,
Unable to see right from wrong.
Boldly standing comfortably,
Unaware you don't belong.

Engaged you think is a busy line,
And not a connection of the brain.
Lacking respect for the rules,
Although you run you are actually lame.

Lacking consideration,
As you greedily eat your cake
Your self centred ways and blindness,
Are in fact your biggest mistake.

"Lost"

In an ivory tower you sit and hide,
Untrusting, protecting your pride.
Mistakes and minefields, live and learn,
Honesty and friendship tables turn.

Acquisition and achievements,
Build stockpiles and protect.
The person behind the bars of steel,
Lacking normality and neglect.

High up and counting,
A challenge to come down.
Practice the smile,
That sits behind the frown.

The spiral staircase down is daunting,
Concentration looking for strength.
Having not looked down when you climbed so high,
Undeterred by time and length.

Using moats as a deterrent,
Mazes an insurance to confuse.
Lifetime lost in foreplay,
Prerogative to choose.

"False Start"

Wanting to run before you can walk,
Frustrated at being unable to talk.
Seeing the finishing line before the start,
Barbed wire to protect the heart.

Feeling the rhythm but unable to move,
Wanting to make a decision but unable to choose.
Taking one step forward ending up two steps back,
Wanting to break free, but confidence lacks.

Arriving at the bus stop, just as it pulls away,
Putting off until tomorrow what you can do today.
Things to be confronted but cannot be faced.
Feelings you have been unable to place.

"Such Caper"

I see your life as a crossword puzzle,
And you are struggling with the clues.
Determined not to admit defeat,
Left in limbo, what to do.

Personality used as a camouflage,
Disguising the frustration you feel inside.
Joviality and wit used to suppress,
Feelings of hurt and anger you hide.

Youthful caper- vocabulary sparse,
Lacking strength to look behind your mask.
Uneasy with responsibility at stalemate stable,
Forward thinking are you able?

"Opportunity Knocking"

Driven by opportunity,
Purpose and a goal.
Seeking direction,
To fill a missing hole.

Mastering to perfection,
Comes at a price.
Overcoming obstacles,
Motivating to entice.

Landmarks and legislation,
Words of wisdom from the wise.
An achievement to conquer,
A trophy or a prize.

Seeking financial rewards,
Requiring money to buy what?
What you are chasing,
Have you already got?

"Too long"

To have been married to that man,
For so many a year.
Who did not often bring you happiness,
But many a tear.

Did you think you had the power,
To change the way he was?
Or had you made your bed,
And lay on it just because?

To live amongst anger and abuse,
With no offer of support.
In his eyes on your wedding day,
You were a purchase he had bought.

Often ordering and yelling at you,
As you tried to keep the peace.
Eager to always be on top,
Grateful to lie beneath.

Although eventually breaking free,
Do you think it was too late?
Children although now grown up,
Left scarred and in an emotional state.

"Half or Whole"

He is your husband,
But do you have any control?
Does he give you enough
To make you feel whole?

Money no object,
Go out and spend.
Knocking your confidence,
Unable to mend.

How much do you want him?
Is it real love?
Do you feel small and low,
As he towers above?

Indulging in sexual activity,
Is the price you pay.
Although he has no interest,
In a word that you say.

Buying presents for yourself,
Taking advantage of his wealth.
Would you prefer an admiring look,
And given back what has been took?

Caught up in dilemma,
Wanting to regain control.
Begrudgingly giving your body,
Holding back your soul.

"Take Cover"

A storm is brewing,
The clouds are up above.
The friction in the house,
Caused by the one she loves.

The storm is getting closer,
The thunder is not far away.
Trying to avoid a brewing situation,
She keeps out of the way and prays.

The lightening strikes,
A dancing crackle in the sky.
His fingers tap the table,
She asks herself why.

A major outburst,
As the thunder shouts and swears.
Actions behind closed doors,
Again her heart tears.

In between the thunderstorms,
She waits for sunshine to arrive.
Glossing over the odd shower,
Just until the next time.

"Sole Trader"

Breaking up is never easy,
A partnership or friend.
Different directions,
Come to an end.

Emotional outbursts,
Preservation is wrong.
Two way traffic,
Togetherness gone.

Difference in opinion,
Lacking insight.
Outrageous behaviour,
Physical fight.

Loosening of links,
Trust or treason.
Forgot the rhyme,
Sure of the reason.

Controlling situations,
Anger and pain.
Solely standing,
Staying sane.

Single ticket,
Ticket to ride.
No longer willing,
To excuse or hide.

"Rattlesnake"

Don't continue to aim your aggression at me,
Are you listening to what I say?
My words are full of truth and honesty,
I'm determined to make you pay.

Life to you is down to payment and bribery,
Happiness runs parallel to wealth and money.
You are close to feeling the sting from the bee,
As I am no longer willing to make the honey.

Face to face you accommodate and smile,
Changing your tune when out of sight.
At ease as you camouflage and slither
So low down and ready to bite

Analyse each situation,
Count your friends- they are few.
You wouldn't be brave enough to do this,
You don't understand the word true.

"Red sky in the morning"

Don't mince your words,
Or knead without reason.
Let loose your emotions,
This is not warfare and treason.

Don't disguise the taste,
If the quality is good.
Getting away with things,
Just because you could.

Prepare and master,
Enjoy the event.
Take note to analyse,
What it has all meant.

Boil then simmer,
Add a little to taste.
Don't be slapdash,
And act in haste.

Preparing and experimenting,
To get it just right.
Enjoying the build up,
And an unimaginable sight.

To over indulge may ruin,
Too much of a good thing.
With the statistics against you,
Should you purchase the ring?

"Suit and unsuitable"

I am what you have made me,
Although you are not what I want to be.
When it suits you totally disregard me,
When it's to your advantage it's 'we'.

Through weakness you choose not to see,
The strength I have and what I could be.
Through insecurity holding me back,
Taking the easy option is how you react.

Always wanting me to wipe your nose,
It's not such a difficult task.
When under pressure you act self righteous,
But I know what's behind your mask.

You are not as good as many think you are,
There is more weakness to you than strength.
By me always being there for you,
Keeps the pretence going for greater length.

Not forthcoming with encouragement,
Emotionally you are cold.
When you are faced with criticism,
Your superiority takes hold.

Stand tall and move forward,
A child you are not.
Unfortunately although you have the words,
Delivery is what you are not.

"Careful of the thorns"

Strong in character, outgoing personality,
Although appearing confident sometimes lost.
Maybe you have already been found,
And are creating confusion at a cost.

Your exterior is hard,
Protective of your space.
But inside I know,
You are ribbons and lace.

Not expecting a bed of roses,
You have known the thorn in the stem.
Wanting to smell the scent of the rose,
But not be hurt so much again.

Very wary of strangers,
Not letting them close enough to touch.
I understand your past,
Has affected you so much.

To unconditionally give and remain patient,
How patient are you expected to be?
Your eyes are now open,
Clear vision makes you able to see.

An ending can be a beginning,
However, each could be at a cost.
I'll always have a map at hand,
To assist you if you are lost.

"Intrigued"

It's always a challenge,
To get into one's head.
Listening carefully,
To what's being said.

It can sometimes be difficult,
If one is trying to hide.
Expert at listening,
To get you on side.

Slowly as you open,
I slip inside the door.
It's not an attempted burglary,
I'm not breaking the law.

To concentrate and scheme,
Very much deep in thought.
Unaware of the situation,
You have sold and I have bought.

Once I know what makes you tick,
I slowly let you know,
Many wouldn't know I've been.
Or be brave enough to go.

"Religion"

Are we punished for things done wrong?
Should we always be willing to sing his song?
What about forgiveness, how often can he forgive?
Not reading his word or the life chosen to live.

Does he always listen,
When we say a prayer?
If you are not reading his word,
Does he pay attention and care?

Would he help with material things,
Such as extras in life?
Well he managed to feed the five thousand,
What about the starving family, child, husband and wife?

Many religions and biblical translations to read,
A society empowered by success and greed.
Adam and Eve the first two on earth,
We are the descendants, what is truly our worth?

If religion provides a security,
For each one of us to grasp,
A nation of believers,
An incredible task.

Questions I ask and need a reply,
Always ending in why-why-why?
Starting with Our Father and ending in Amen,
Tomorrow we will say this all over again.

Knock-Knock is anybody there?

"Acceptance"

I hear you calling,
But I can't speak.
Exterior strong,
Inside weak.

I see you in the distance,
But I can't grasp.
In slow motion,
As you move too fast.

I read your words,
But mentally withdraw.
Realising I'm at battle,
An unexpected war.

I'm aware of your presence,
But I choose not to feel.
Keeping at a safe distance
Until I can accept that you are real.

"Knock, Knock"

Knock, Knock, is anybody there?
I've been knocking so long, I don't think you care.
Since I knit you together in your mother's womb
I've been longing to be your saviour – but do you have the room?

Every morning with the sunrise, every evening as it sets
I tell you that I love you – will you listen yet?
So frightened of being punished for things done wrong
Have you still not heard that forgiveness is my song?

If you ask you will receive, if you seek you will find
And when you knock, I promise, the door will open every time.
Are you frightened of receiving, are you worried what you may find?
When you knock, do you really want to meet me, or do you run away
and hide?

Are you hiding from my presence,
Are you hiding from my grace?
My daughter, I sent my son
So we could see face to face.

Hiding behind questions, be they big or be they small
But you know that if you read my word you'd find the answers to
them all.
Take off the blinkers, come out of the night
When you see as I see you can walk in the light.

I am the great provider, I will take care of all you need,
I give the sun that shines on a world obsessed with greed.
How would you like to pay, ma'am, cash, credit card or cheque?
No-one has put a price on the gift of sun and air just yet.

Leave the world behind, with all its lies and shattered dreams
You know it won't fulfil, only rip apart at the seams.
For how much will it profit you, if that is your goal,
If you gain all the world has to offer, but forfeit your soul.

My call is not easy, lose your life for me
The road is not easy, it's the narrow gate you see.

I ask you to be perfect, that's why you need the cross
That's why I came to look for you, to seek and save the lost.

So look, I stand here knocking, will you ask me in?
If you hear my voice I'll eat with you, and take away your sin.
My daughter, you're so precious, I died for you alone
So now I wait for your reply – I want to take you home.

Written by Julie Wanstall

Silks

"Is this it?"

What is love,
Is it a feeling?
Is it an apple,
That you are peeling?

Having seen the exterior,
Are you intrigued to get inside?
Are you using a camouflage,
What are you trying to hide?

Does it feel like a summer evening,
Light nights and feeling jolly?
Does it feel like winter,
Surrounded by berries and holly?

Can you explain love,
By the taste and by the smell?
What are you asking for,
At the wishing well?

Do your eyelids flutter?
Do your eyes shine bright?
Does your heart skip a beat,
At the thought or at the sight?

Is this the love,
That you feel comfortable with and know?
Are you watering and nurturing,
And waiting for it to grow?

"Blink or Wink"

Confidently you're standing there,
Daring to look my way.
Concentrating on the music,
Allowing my body to sway.

A smirk portraying self assurance,
A smile or was it a grin?
Certainly using your ace card,
Determined to play and win.

To catch my eye and hold my gaze,
A deep and penetrating stare.
Daring to think what is underneath,
The immaculate clothes you wear.

To touch my hand to hold and grip,
Guiding me closer to you.
Feeling unsure at this moment,
Of what's expected and what to do.

Remaining confident and standing,
Face to face and looking my way.
No longer hearing the music,
But allowing my body to sway.

"Dig deep"

Our newness together is exciting,
I can't control the turbulence inside.
Outside confidently beaming,
Head held high with pride.

Dates and destinations,
Labelled as a pair.
Building upon foundations,
Showing creative flair.

Friends and familiarity,
Introductions to entice.
Bad habits on the back burner,
Showing a side as cool as ice.

Hands to hold and wander,
How far may they go?
Respecting you immensely,
Trying hard to take it slow.

"Sweet"

Remembering what you wore,
Watching your every move.
Did we win?
Or maybe lose.

Winning is an achievement,
Are you willing to play?
'I'm in a rush',
I heard you say.

Where were you rushing?
Did I just bore?
Having tasted the apple,
I know you wanted the core.

They say the meat is sweeter,
Nearer to the bone.
Don't just walk away from me,
I want to take you home.

"Dinner for two"

Sit at my table,
Eat my food.
For your sweet,
Talk to me rude.

Dirty dishes,
Sexual wishes.
Soapy water,
Someone's daughter.

Forget the breakfast,
Get back in bed.
Just love being,
So easily led.

Empty teacups,
Kettle switched off.
A doctor's appointment,
Instructed to cough.

Lunch or lunchbox,
Box of tricks
A tongue to taste,
That also licks.

Sit at my table,
Dinner is served.
Providing you,
With what you deserve.

"Association"

Why associate yourself with me,
I am clearly cut against the grain.
In my eyes you are perfection,
My inadequacies at times a strain.

Slightly rough around the edge,
At times as sharp as a knife.
However you say you could trust me,
With something as precious as your life.

Split ends and personality,
Tears of a clown.
Giving me the strength,
When I'm feeling down.

Unpredictable in character,
At times irrational and perverse.
I am your heartbeat,
You the minister of my verse.

"Ruler or Tape"

An instant attraction,
A feeling, a spark.
A smile, a sparkle,
A flutter from the heart.

A right one, a wrong one.
But is wrong sometimes right?
Could a gentle exterior
Be ready to bite?

A broker, a builder, boots or brogues,
A flat hat, a hard hat, a pencil or pen
What you want now
Did you want then?

All a means to an end,
Or is it an end to a means?
Are you enjoying fresh bread and butter
Or stale bread and cheese?

A feeling, a sparkle,
A candle burning.
A man, a woman,
A continual yearning.

To give, to take, to love, to hate.
Today, tomorrow, yesterday, next week.
Until the heart
Ceases to beat.

"Proof"

Your cockiness and naivety amuses me,
In your company I'm at ease and love to be.
Laid back and unsure of where you are going,
My feelings for you are definitely growing.

A sparkle bounces between our eyes,
Chemistry calling, never questioning why.
An opportunity a brand new start,
Wanting to get inside and listen to your heart.

Intrigued by such dominance but it also scares,
Worried if by revealing your heart will tear.
Speculate to accumulate- place your bet,
Panicking in case your ways are set.

Moving forward then to suddenly backtrack,
Are you worried that experience you lack?
Painting by numbers one step at a time,
Continuation or to decline?

"A waste of Space"

A waste of time and effort,
Time which could be better spent.
Missing parts of the evening,
Wondering where the time went.

Not knowing your name,
Or the rules of your game.
But with you spending time,
Willingly crossing the line.

Reminded of activities,
That I am assured took place.
Ashamed I can't even,
Remember your face.

"Hands"

Holding hands,
Fingers entwined.
For this short moment,
You feel as if you are mine.

A tingling feeling,
The sensation of your touch.
Revealing to me,
More than enough.

The security of your hardness,
Which is softened by your stroke.
So gentle in character,
When not being provoked.

Hands for working,
Hands for play.
Hands that can speak volumes,
No words to say.

In contrast to a formal handshake,
Accompanying hello and goodbye.
No arousing feeling,
No expiratory sigh.

The same hand unfortunately,
Could decide to wave goodbye.
I'll be smiling back at you,
Will I smile or will I cry?

105

"The Lyrics"

Losing control I unintentionally trip,
Realising I have let my guard slip.
Knowing that I have fallen for you,
Unsure of what next I should do.

Fully aware I am now in a trap,
Maybe a predetermined mishap.
Emotions revealed a twinkle in my eyes,
Unable any longer to hide behind a disguise.

Aware of the spring in my step,
Also in the way my heart leapt.
My face has a certain glow,
How soon and fast will it go?

Excitably calm,
As I hold onto his arm
No appetite to eat,
Watching me from the opposite seat.

Too scared to sprint,
Preferring to jog along.
Carefully collating the words,
To complete and master the song.

"Trekking"

Again familiarity calls,
Breaking all the rules.
Flirtatious banter feeling good,
Ambiguous clues understood.

Controlling emotions a hard task,
Questions to be addressed and asked.
Excuses denial to walk away,
Unable to withdraw from play.

Attention seeking a two sided coin,
Consenting in silence together to join.
Eyes are closing to blindly advance,
Time standing still a tantalising trance.

To hanker after but anxious to move on,
Aware we are singing two different songs.
The chorus familiar but short and sweet,
Are our pathways destined to meet?

"Chit Chat"

I think I have feelings for you,
I am unsure just how real.
I'm frustrated that I am unable,
To express in voice how I feel.

Communicating via technology,
Starting as relaxing banter and fun.
But you are now permanently in my head,
Do you realise what you have done?

Having never met in person,
Relying on portraits in our heads.
Words so wise and witty,
Through laughter I am led.

Distantly demanding,
But a switch maintains control.
Muddling along on half measures,
Wondering about you as a whole.

"Frosty"

Feelings can't be put into words,
No explanation for how you feel.
Are you sure your feelings are not fabricated?
Are you sure they are real?

Pressure building up,
Far too much too soon.
Is there enough space?
Is there any room?

A volcano waiting to erupt,
Choosing its own time.
Arrogance and aggression enticing lightening,
When the weather was perfectly fine.

To hold on not wanting to let go,
But you know the moment may come.
Are you holding the bullet in your hand?
Too scared to place in the gun.

Why the attraction in a stinging nettle,
You know a dock leaf will soothe.
Have you the strength to conquer?
When there's a good chance you could lose.

Feelings can't be put into words,
But you know inside how you feel.
Knowing that what you feel is not fabricated,
Knowing what you feel is real.

"Time out"

The peace and quiet,
The still of the night.
Focusing on the moonlight,
Such a tranquil sight.

I want you to share this experience,
Don't be scared to take my hand.
Unveiling emotions,
Toes wriggling in the sand.

I hear the heartbeat of the music,
But it's only in my head.
Listening oh so carefully,
To the words that are said.

Engulfed by the ripple of the trees,
Stroked by the night-time breeze.
Tranquillity as the tide comes in,
The heart can't help but sing.

The stars demanding my attention,
Before the sunrise takes centre stage.
Enjoying the excitement of the build up,
But too eager to turn the page.

"There and where"

Subconsciously you are often there,
In reality I have never seen.
Looking for you in times of trouble,
A shoulder on which I can lean.

Uninvited you enter my mind,
When I am at peace and fast asleep.
In the morning I wonder if you're still there,
When I cautiously decide to peep.

Although I see you in the distance,
Arms outstretched I am unable to touch.
In my head we frequently meet,
But it is just an illusion as such.

Sometimes deciding on an early night,
So with you I can spend more time.
Preparing myself for your visits,
As if in reality you are mine.

So angry when I am woken,
It always feels too soon.
Even if time is sometimes short,
I accommodate to give you room.

Feeling let down and disappointed,
When you choose not to call.
Waiting in anticipation,
When I am able to give you all.

"This or That"

Call or caller,
Ring or rung.
Sing or singer,
The song's been sung.

Lonely or loneliness,
Loneliness in love.
Love or lust,
A lustful must.

Tears or teardrops,
Tears of joy.
Joy and laughter,
Smirk so coy.

Heartbeat and butterflies,
Butterflies so free.
Free from emotion,
Too emotional for me.

Eyes for winking,
Winking to attract.
Attraction looking for action,
Action to attack.

Cuddles and affection,
To be affectionate and true.
How true am I to I?
How true are you to you?

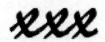